Louisa Catherine Johnson Adams

Louisa Catherine Johnson Adams

* *

1775–1852

BY ANN HEINRICHS

CHILDREN'S PRESS®
A Division of Grolier Publishing
New York   London   Hong Kong   Sydney
Danbury, Connecticut

Consultants: JOHN STANWICH
                 Park Ranger, Historian
                 Adams National Historic Site
                 Quincy, Massachusetts
                 LINDA CORNWELL
                 Learning Resource Consultant
                 Indiana Department of Education

Project Editor: DOWNING PUBLISHING SERVICES
Page Layout: CAROLE DESNOES
Photo Researcher: JAN IZZO

Visit Children's Press on the Internet at:
http://publishing.grolier.com

Library of Congress Cataloging-in-Publication Data
Heinrichs, Ann
       Louisa Catherine Johnson Adams, 1775–1852 / by Ann Heinrichs
          p. cm. — (Encyclopedia of first ladies)
       Includes bibliographical references and index.
       Summary: A biography of the wife of the sixth president of the United States,
    discussing her childhood, marriage, and social activities at the White House.
       ISBN 0-516-20845-4
       1. Adams, Louisa Catherine, 1775–1852—Juvenile literature. 2. Presidents' spouses—
    United States—Biography—Juvenile literature. [1. Adams, Louisa Catherine, 1775–1852.
    2. First ladies.   3. Women—Biography.] I. Title.
    E377.2.H4   1998
    793.5'5'092—dc21   97-47279
    [B]   CIP
                                                                AC

Table of Contents

Louisa Catherine Johnson Adams

CHAPTER ONE

Terror on the French Frontier

★ ☆ ★ ☆ ★ ☆ ★ ☆ ★ ☆ ★ ☆ ★ ☆ ★ ☆ ★ ☆ ★ ☆ ★

"Tear them out of the carriage!"

Drunken French soldiers grabbed the horses' reins. Huddled inside the carriage was Louisa Adams, pale as a ghost.

The sight of Louisa's Russian-style carriage drove the Frenchmen wild. Not one had forgotten France's bitter defeat in Russia. Now Napoleon, their fallen emperor, was on his way back from exile. His old army would soon be in power again. They were not about to let a Russian coach pass them by.

"Take them out! Kill them!" snarled the ragtag troops, raising their rifles to fire. Meanwhile, safe in his

★ ☆ ★ ☆ ★ ☆ ★ ☆ ★ ☆ ★ ☆ ★ ☆ ★ ☆ ★ ☆ ★ ☆ ★

Name That Country

★ ★

It may seem strange, but from history's point of view, countries come and go. During the time Louisa lived in Europe, the countries there were quite different than they are today. Does the Kingdom of Prussia sound strange to you? This ancient empire took up much of northern Europe. The Austrian Empire occupied central Europe. In the south, where Greece and Turkey are today, the powerful Ottoman Empire ruled. Germany was not yet a nation but a collection of about three hundred independent states. Italy was made up of a dozen or so kingdoms and republics, such as the Kingdom of Naples and the Papal States. To the east, the mighty Russian Empire loomed. And in France, the brilliant leader Napoleon rose to power and hoped to bring all of Europe under his rule. For ordinary Europeans, wars and revolutions around the continent made life dangerous at worst and uncertain at best.

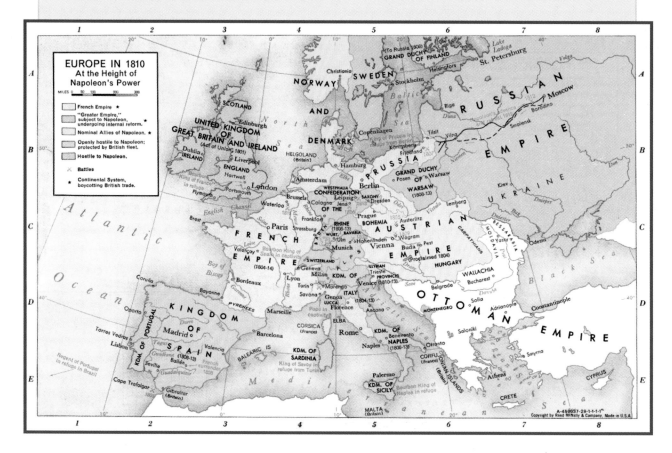

Paris hotel, John Quincy Adams wondered what was taking his wife so long.

The wild-eyed mob swarmed closer, jostling one another to peer inside. Louisa clutched her little son Charles tighter. On the opposite seat, Madame Babet, her maid, whimpered and sobbed.

Louisa must have wondered how she had sunk so far, so fast. Just weeks ago, she was waltzing in the palace of St. Petersburg. Before that, she was the darling of Berlin. At Charles's age, she had lived in a castle, like a fairytale princess in a little girl's dream.

But the last few weeks had been a nightmare. Louisa had crossed icy rivers, hidden from hostile armies, and trudged up to her ankles in mud. Only the thought of her husband drew her on.

Now, just a few days away from Paris, Louisa faced the guns of a vicious mob. Would it all end here?

☆ ☆ ☆ ☆ ☆ ☆ ☆ ☆ ☆ ☆ ☆ ☆ ☆ ☆ ☆

CHAPTER TWO

Growing Up in Europe

☆ ☆ ☆ ☆ ☆ ☆ ☆ ☆ ☆ ☆ ☆ ☆ ☆ ☆ ☆ ☆ ☆

Louisa Catherine Johnson was born on February 12, 1775. Her father, Joshua Johnson, had grown up in the Maryland Colony. As a young man, he had founded a shipping company and sailed to London. There, he met Catherine Nuth, who was one of twenty-two children. At the age of sixteen, she married Joshua Johnson. Soon, their daughter Nancy was born. Fourteen months later, Louisa arrived.

Catherine loved to entertain. In the evenings, the Johnson home was filled with guests. Delicate, witty, and dressed in laces and silk, Catherine was a sparkling hostess. Joshua adored his wife. When she was sick, he

☆ ☆ ☆ ☆ ☆ ☆ ☆ ☆ ☆ ☆ ☆ ☆ ☆ ☆ ☆ ☆ ☆

Portrait of America, 1775: Up in Arms

☆ ☆

In the same year that Louisa Johnson was born in London, revolution was brewing across the Atlantic Ocean in America. The thirteen colonies wanted their independence from England, and by 1775, war seemed unavoidable. Even on the eve of revolution, however, life went on. Most Americans lived on farms. Only 5 percent of the population lived in the cities. The first American surgical textbook was published in 1775, and the first daily newspaper was printed in Philadelphia. Benjamin Franklin reorganized the post office, and the colonies provided much of the world's supply of iron. While most Americans lived along the Atlantic seaboard, explorers began to push into the vast western wilderness.

The year 1775 is remembered best as the first year of the American Revolution. On April 18, British troops began a march from Boston to seize a store of weapons at Concord. That night, Paul Revere alerted the countryside that the "British were coming." Four thousand minutemen—farmers and townsfolk trained to turn out at a moment's notice—rushed from their beds to attack British troops. No one knows who fired the first shot on the village green at Lexington, but it was "heard round the world" because it signaled the start of war. Battles followed along the road as the British retreated back to Boston.

In May, Congress authorized a Continental army of 20,000 under the leadership of George Washington. Most people supported the revolution, but, just like today, Americans disagreed with one another. Friends, neighbors, and families split over the issues of war and independence. Some colonists, called Tories, remained loyal to Britain. Congress tried to win the support of Native Americans, but many tribes who felt pressured by white settlers to give up their lands sided with the British. Two thousand African slaves seeking their own liberty enlisted with the British who promised them freedom in exchange. For American women, 1775 brought a personal kind of independence. As husbands, sons, and fathers went off to war, women remained behind to run the farms and businesses.

After the American Revolution began, the Johnsons moved to Nantes, France, a seaport on the Loire River.

sat by her bedside. He did not seem to mind spending money on her parties.

More than 3,000 miles (4,828 kilometers) away, the American colonies were ready to go to war for their freedom from Great Britain. Two months after Louisa was born, the American Revolution began. On July 4, 1776, colonists signed a Declaration of Independence.

Joshua listened excitedly to news from the colonies. He and Catherine began to feel uneasy, though. As an American in England, Joshua was living on enemy soil. In 1778, the Johnsons packed up their family and sailed to safety in France. They settled in Nantes, a seaport on the Loire River.

"I perfectly remember the elegance

The American Revolution: Fast Facts

WHAT: The war for American independence

WHEN: 1775–1783

WHO: Between Britain and the thirteen American colonies. France and Spain joined the war in support of the colonies in 1778.

WHERE: Along the east coast of North America, and as far west as Indiana, with major battles in Massachusetts, New York, New Jersey, Pennsylvania, the Carolinas, Virginia, and Canada.

WHY: Began as a dispute between colonists and king over Britain's authority and its power to tax and control trade in the American colonies. On July 4, 1776, when leading American patriots signed the Declaration of Independence, everything changed. Now, the colonists were fighting for their independence from Britain.

OUTCOME: An American victory at Yorktown, Virginia, ended the fighting, but it took two more years for a treaty to be signed. Finally, in 1783, England recognized the United States of America with the Treaty of Paris.

On special occasions, Louisa's mother dressed her in silk dresses with big hoop skirts, the latest in fashion for young girls in France.

From the windows, Louisa could watch ships sailing up and down the Loire. Bridges connected all the islands to one another, and rows of houses lined the shore. On the mainland, broad meadows shimmered in the sun.

"My earliest recollections are French," Louisa wrote. With her nurse as a coach, she soon spoke excellent French. When she was old enough, she attended a Catholic convent school run by nuns. On special occasions, Louisa's mother dressed her in the latest style. For a little girl in France, this meant silk dresses with big hoop skirts.

Joshua often welcomed visiting Americans to his home. One day in 1779, an important congressman from Massachusetts arrived. It was John Adams, with his eleven-year-old son John Quincy. Did young John Quincy and four-year-old Louisa notice each other? No one knows. Years later, after their marriage, old John Adams wrote to his son Thomas: "I suppose this match grew out of a

of the mansion in which we resided," Louisa later wrote. The Johnsons' home was like a huge stone castle. It was perched on one of the many islands scattered at the river's mouth.

John Adams as he looked about the time he visited the Johnson family in France.

John Quincy Adams at the age of twelve, shortly after he met Louisa

Spark that was kindled at Nantes in 1779 when your Brother was with me frequently in the Family of Mr. Johnson."

When the war ended in 1783, the Johnsons returned to London. They moved into an elegant house in Cooper's Row on Tower Hill. By 1787, the family had grown to seven girls and one boy. On Sunday mornings, Catherine dressed them all alike and marched them to church, two by two.

Louisa and her sisters were sent to a young ladies' boarding school. Because of their "deep and utter ignorance of English," Louisa later wrote, they were "objects of ridicule to the whole school." Louisa became gloomy and kept to herself, but this only made things worse. The other girls called her "Miss Proud."

Louisa became close to only one of her schoolmates. She was a girl from India who had dark skin and long black hair. Like Louisa, she was quiet and loved to read. The two shared a room, read books together, and were almost inseparable.

Louisa lived for vacation time. The girls loved to play dress-up in their mother's gowns. Louisa always pretended to be a duchess and insisted that everyone call her "Your Grace."

In 1790, Joshua was appointed American consul in London. Louisa, then fifteen, was becoming a pretty young lady. She was slender and delicate with green eyes and auburn curls. While her sister Nancy was bubbly and outgoing, Louisa was more reserved. She played the piano and harp and enjoyed quiet afternoons of reading and writing poetry. In Louisa's mind, "music and reading were the only things in life I thought worth living for."

When the girls were old enough, they were allowed to attend the Johnsons' evening parties. Louisa often entertained the guests with her music and poems. The young bachelors of London could not help noticing the lovely Johnson girls.

One day, Joshua received a stern letter from his brother Thomas, now the governor of Maryland. News of the popular Johnson girls had drifted all the way back to the United States.

Take care, Thomas warned his brother. The girls must not get too

London, England

* *

Louisa Johnson is the only First Lady in history to be born outside America. London, the capital of England, was her birthplace in 1775, and she spent the first three years of her life there. George III, a dull-witted king with few skills as a leader, ruled England then. However, in spite of him and trouble with the colonies in America, London was a growing, bustling city in the late eighteenth century. Located on the great river Thames, it was a center of commerce, shipping, and industry. In this time of great learning and scientific curiosity, as well as literary and artistic accomplishment, well-to-do families such as Louisa's led elegant lives surrounded by lovely furniture and art. Fashions were extravagant, too, especially for clothes worn in the evening. Stylish women wore hoops under their skirts so large that they might not fit through doorways. They piled their heads high with elaborate wigs tall enough to make passing under chandeliers a hazard. Men dressed flamboyantly as well, in colorful fabrics and silk stockings.

Stylish London women of the 1780s wore wide hoop skirts and elaborate wigs and headdresses.

When John Quincy Adams was U.S. minister to the Netherlands (above) in 1795, the twenty-seven-year-old man was a frequent visitor to the Johnson family in London.

John Quincy Adams at the age of twenty-seven

friendly with Englishmen. As Americans, they should take up only with proper American men. At once, Joshua clamped down on the girls' social life. Louisa and her sisters pouted about Uncle Thomas's "silly letter," but their father's word was law.

One evening in 1795, a young American came to dinner. It was John Quincy Adams, now twenty-seven years old. His father, Joshua's old friend John, was now the first vice president of the new United States.

John Quincy was serving as U.S. minister to the Netherlands. On trips

Louisa's sister,
Nancy Johnson

to England, he visited the Johnsons many times. Louisa's mother admired the brilliant young diplomat. Joshua did not feel quite the same. As a southern gentleman, he resented northerners, or "Yankees." He said they did not make good husbands.

The girls liked John Quincy but giggled about his odd-looking Dutch-style clothes.

Whenever John Quincy came by, Joshua made the girls play and sing for him. When Louisa sang, she later wrote, her songs were "so disagreeable

Only three months after John Quincy attended Louisa's twenty-first birthday ball, he asked her father for permission to marry her.

to him he would immediately take his hat and bid us good night when I began one of them."

Everyone thought John Quincy had his eye on Nancy, the oldest sister. Louisa felt free to joke with him and tease, just as if he were a brother. Besides, she thought she was not as pretty as her sisters. No one was more surprised than Louisa when John Quincy turned his attentions to her.

In February 1796, John Quincy attended Louisa's twenty-first birthday ball. They danced, and he escorted her around the room on his arm. In the manners of the time, this was a clear sign that the two were a "pair." In May, John Quincy asked Joshua for his permission to marry Louisa. Joshua agreed.

Right away, John Quincy had to rush back to the Netherlands. While

When John Quincy was seven years old and the American Revolution exploded around his home, his mother took him to a hilltop to watch the Battle of Bunker Hill (above).

he was gone, he told Louisa, she needed to improve her mind. He assigned her a reading list. She was to study until they met again, "which might be in one year or in seven."

Louisa hated the thought of a long engagement. People gossiped and joked about engaged women, she said.

She wanted to get married before John Quincy left. Then she could stay with her parents until they could be together. But John Quincy said no.

Many times during their later life together, Louisa ran up against John Quincy's stern, hard-headed attitudes. But John Quincy himself had been brought up sternly. From an early age, his parents stressed duty, learning, and virtue. As the American Revolution exploded around his home, he watched his mother melt down her metal dishes to be made into bullets. When he was seven, she took him to a hilltop to watch the Battle of Bunker Hill. At nine, he was reading heavy volumes of literature and ancient history. At ten, he traveled to Europe with his diplomat father. All the time, he was urged to live up to the Adams family's high values. Louisa's early days had been much more carefree. It is no wonder, then, that the two often clashed.

Joshua rented a house for Louisa that summer, where she could devote herself to her studies. She counted the hours until a letter from John Quincy arrived. Then she was gripped with terror at the thought of writing back. She had her governess correct her letters to give them the right sound.

John Quincy did not say a word about the engagement to his family in Massachusetts. But his mother, Abigail, heard the news anyway. She was totally against the match. Louisa

Abigail Adams, John Quincy's mother, was fully convinced that Louisa Catherine Johnson would not be a proper wife for her son.

had been born and raised in Europe. To Abigail, this made her unfit for American life and a poor wife for John Quincy.

"I would hope for the love I bear my country that the Siren is at least *half-blood*," Abigail wrote. John Quincy's father was more ready to accept Louisa. "I have not a word to say," he wrote to his son. "You are now of age to judge for yourself."

By autumn, there was still no wedding date. Louisa's father was anxious to sail back to Maryland. He had received word that his company was in trouble. Yet, he hated to go without attending Louisa's wedding.

Joshua was worried about Louisa's health, too. She was becoming a nervous wreck. John Quincy's letters were often stern, and he seemed in no hurry to get married. When she wrote that she missed him, he advised her to accept things she could not change.

In the spring of 1797, John Quincy received orders to go to Lisbon, Portugal, as U.S. minister. Get ready for the wedding, he told Louisa. He could spare only a few days in England before rushing on to Lisbon. Louisa's mother flew into a frenzy. She prepared Louisa's wedding dress and clothes for her new life in Portugal. Trunks were packed with care. But weeks passed without any more news from John Quincy.

"Considering it as a false alarm," Louisa wrote, "everything was locked up and all the preparations concealed with as much care as if I had committed some crime in having made them."

John Quincy finally appeared in London on July 12. "I met him with feelings of mortified affection more bitter than I could express," Louisa wrote. She set the wedding date for July 26.

Then John Quincy received a letter from his father. The older Adams had just become the second president of the United States. Instead of going to Lisbon, the letter said, John Quincy was to go to Berlin. There, he would serve as U.S. minister to Prussia.

On the wedding day, John Quincy wore his powdered wig. Louisa's auburn curls peeked out from under a blue-ribboned bonnet. Together, they walked to the Church of All Hallows Barking on Tower Hill. They passed through tall oak doors, stepped into the dimly lit church, and crossed the cool stone floor. Before Reverend John Hewlett, the couple exchanged

For their honeymoon, Louisa and John Quincy traveled around the English countryside in the company of Louisa's maid and John Quincy's brother Thomas.

vows that would bind them together for fifty-one years.

For their honeymoon, the newlyweds traveled around the English countryside. In the custom of the time, they were not alone. Louisa's maid and John Quincy's brother Thomas came along. In November, Louisa, John Quincy, and Thomas set out for Berlin.

★ ★ ★ ★ ★ ★ ★ ★ ★ ★ ★ ★ ★ ★ ★

CHAPTER THREE

Learning to Be Mrs. Adams

☆ ☆ ☆ ☆ ☆ ☆ ☆ ☆ ☆ ☆ ☆ ☆ ☆ ☆ ☆ ☆

Married life was a bit of a shock for Louisa. She missed her parents terribly. Except for her boarding-school days, she had never been apart from her mother. Louisa probably had a rosy view of marriage, too. Her parents had a warm and loving marriage. Even her famous father-in-law had a fond respect for his outspoken wife, Abigail.

In many ways, women of Abigail's age had enjoyed more freedoms. In the rough times before the American Revolution, strong women were prized. They shared in the hard work of building up homes and businesses in the struggling colonies.

☆ ☆ ☆ ☆ ☆ ☆ ☆ ☆ ☆ ☆ ☆ ☆ ☆ ☆ ☆ ☆

Abigail Adams (1744–1818)

✫ ✫

It is no wonder that the sturdy Abigail Adams believed her delicate daughter-in-law Louisa to be unfit for life in America. From August 1774, when her husband, John Adams, left for the First Continental Congress in Philadelphia, Abigail took over the management of his farming and business affairs. At the same time, she continued to run the household and raise and educate their children. She bought farm animals, hired help, dealt with tenants, and expanded their landholdings. In

the 1790s, she directed the farm and dairy down to the last detail from Europe and New York by writing letters to a local agent. "Mr. A.," she wrote, "has been so long a Statesman that I cannot get him to think enough upon his domestick affairs." In letters to her husband, she took to referring to "our farm" instead of "your farm." Thanks to Abigail's skill and hard work, John Adams escaped the financial ruin that overtook so many of his fellow statesmen.

Abigail Adams managed her husband's farm and business affairs while he was involved in the affairs of state.

Once the fighting began, women even followed the troops onto the battlefield. They fetched water, carried ammunition, nursed the wounded, and cooked meals. Meanwhile, women at home sometimes had to shoot British troops who stormed into their homes.

By Louisa's time, however, the country had settled down. In large cities, people took on the social graces of European society. A proper lady kept quiet and behaved sweetly. The good wife was a decoration for her husband and his career.

Louisa learned to keep her opinions to herself. John Quincy severely warned her never to criticize him, especially about his clothes. Years later, she wrote that "hanging and marriage were strongly assimilated."

In addition, a black cloud hung over Louisa's marriage. It was the custom at the time for a bride to have a dowry. This was a gift from the bride's family to the groom. Usually, a dowry consisted of money or property or both. Of course, it was not polite for a man to have his eye on a woman's dowry. Still, a good woman with a good dowry was a "better catch" than just a good woman.

Joshua had promised Louisa a sizeable dowry of five thousand British pounds. When he finally reached Maryland, however, he found that his company had collapsed. Now penniless, Joshua could offer Louisa nothing. He could not even pay his London bills. Worse still, his creditors began hounding John Quincy to pay them.

Louisa was shattered. For the rest of her life, she never forgot this humiliation. "The injury which Mr. A. received by his marriage with me," she wrote, "was the loss of the five thousand pounds . . . and having connected himself with a ruined house."

In Berlin, Louisa and John rented a small, inexpensive apartment. Louisa sewed curtains for their home and dresses for herself. For the first year, the couple could not even afford a coach. (In today's terms, having a coach was like having a car.)

Berlin's social life gave Louisa a chance to enjoy herself. Almost every evening, there were operas, dinners, and balls. Louisa made friends easily

Revolutionary Women

✶ ✶

Many patriotic American women pitched in to help during the Revolutionary War. The most famous of these women was undoubtedly "Molly Pitcher." Given that nickname because she carried water to the soldiers on the front lines, Mary Hays McCauley took her husband's place loading a cannon when he fainted from the heat during the Battle of Monmouth. Deborah Sampson fought disguised as a man for more than a year when she served under the name Robert Shurtleff in the Continental army. Her husband became the only man to receive a pension as a "widow" of a Revolutionary War soldier. While many women stayed home to run the farms, some women traveled with their soldier husbands from battlefield to battlefield, cooking and sewing for them. Making a less dangerous contribution were the Philadelphia women who formed a committee to raise funds for the soldiers by going door to door. Heading up this effort was Esther Reed, wife of the governor of Pennsylvania. She published an article titled "Sentiments of an American Woman" that encouraged women throughout the colonies to organize fundraising campaigns.

Molly Pitcher loaded a cannon in her husband's place during the Battle of Monmouth.

and became a favorite of Prussia's king and queen. John Quincy grumbled about life in Berlin. He did not care for parties or dancing, so his brother Thomas often escorted Louisa.

One day, the queen gave Louisa a jar of rouge. Louisa knew that John Quincy, with his strict religious upbringing, was opposed to makeup. Still, she thought she looked terribly pale. One night before they went out, Louisa dared to apply a little rouge to her cheeks. When she met John Quincy at the front door, he became enraged. He demanded that she wash it off, but she refused. Then he sat her down, got a wet towel, and scrubbed her cheeks. Louisa cried, then they kissed and made up.

On another evening, she defiantly applied the rouge again. John Quincy took one look, then jumped into the coach and left without her. Louisa followed, alone, in another carriage.

When she arrived in Berlin, Louisa was expecting her first baby. Only a month later, she had a miscarriage. She and John Quincy were broken-hearted. Over the next three years, Louisa became pregnant four more times. Each pregnancy ended in a miscarriage.

At that time, miscarriages were much more common than they are today. Also, without modern medical care, many women died during child-birth. Women's health in the 1800s was generally poor. For one thing, people did not realize how important diet and exercise are for good health. Sports and vigorous athletic activities were considered too unladylike for women and girls.

Women's clothing affected their health, too. Fashionable women wore tightly laced undergarments that made their waists look small. But these corsets also made it hard for women to move freely or even to breathe normally. It is no wonder that many women in Louisa's time were not strong or healthy enough to have children.

Finally, in April 1801, Louisa gave birth to a baby boy. He was named George Washington Adams. Two months later, John Quincy was called back to the United States. Louisa, still weak from childbirth, could hardly walk. In their fifty-eight days at sea,

Louisa's new life in rustic America, with its unpaved roads and unfinished cities, was a stark contrast to her first twenty-six years in the fashionable cities of Europe. Just before she and John Quincy traveled to his home in Massachusetts, they were living in Berlin, where Louisa strolled in the Tiergarten (above) and shopped in the Market Place (below).

little George was so sick she thought he would die. Nevertheless, they arrived safely at the port of Philadelphia, and Louisa stepped ashore.

After living in Europe for twenty-six years, everything in America seemed strange to Louisa. She could hardly eat the food, and people's speech sounded crude. Traveling meant violent stagecoach rides on rocky, muddy roads. That was how Louisa and John Quincy got to the Adams family home in Quincy, Massachusetts. Louisa was dismayed at the sight of her husband's rustic hometown. "Had I stepp'd into Noah's ark,"

Half the Fun?

✶ ✶

In the days when Louisa was traveling back and forth to Europe, there was no easy way to transport passengers across the Atlantic. Although the ocean teemed with tall-masted sailing ships—trading ships, mail packets, whalers, slave ships, pirate ships, and naval brigs—no passenger vessels plied the waters until 1816. Some 19,000 traders left from British ports alone in 1811. Warfare in Europe and America spilled onto the high seas after 1803, making ocean crossings treacherous and discouraging the establishment of passenger liners. Therefore, people wishing to travel overseas took their chances on any ship that would carry them. Some ships, built for speed with tall masts, were unstable enough to capsize. Others were so crowded that conditions on board could turn deadly as passengers became sick or food and water ran out. The journey westward generally took more than 50 days (prevailing winds made an eastward trip quicker), but weather conditions made travel times unpredictable. Overpowering storms and maddening calms might make any voyage miserable. For Louisa, who made three transatlantic crossings and spent a total of well over 100 days at sea, getting there was probably not half the fun.

The Adamses' tall-masted sailing ship finally arrived at the port of Philadelphia in the late summer of 1801 after 58 days at sea.

Louisa, John Quincy, and baby George traveled from Philadelphia to Quincy by stagecoach—a long, rough journey over rocky, muddy roads.

The Adams family home in Quincy, Massachusetts

When Louisa and John Quincy arrived in Washington, D.C., the city looked more like a rural town than the capital of a new nation.

she wrote, "I do not think I could have been more utterly astonished."

At last, Louisa found herself face-to-face with her mother-in-law, Abigail. Louisa, thin and pale, seemed just as Abigail had expected—completely unfit for life in the United States. Yet the two treated each other as politely as possible.

In February 1803, the Massachusetts legislature selected John Quincy to serve in the U.S. Senate. On the Fourth of July, as he packed for

their trip to the capital, Louisa had another baby boy. They named him John Adams, after his grandfather.

Louisa called Washington a "scene of utter desolation." Pennsylvania Avenue, the main street, was muddy and full of holes. Farmyards and wooden houses were scattered here and there. Cows and horses grazed on the lawns and pigs wandered in the streets.

Louisa and John Quincy could not afford a house of their own. Instead,

In 1806, John Quincy bought a house in Boston, only a few miles from the Adams family home in Quincy, and began giving lectures at Harvard College (above).

they moved in with Louisa's sister and brother-in-law, Nancy and Walter Hellen. The house was 5 miles (8 km) outside of town, and John Quincy walked to work at the Capitol every day.

Congress met from December through May. John Quincy spent summers with his family, often leaving Louisa behind in Washington. In 1805, he decided that their two little sons would be left with his mother in Quincy. Abigail believed that Washington was not a good place for them. It broke Louisa's heart to part with her babies, but no one had asked her opinion.

The next year, John Quincy bought a house in Boston and began giving lectures at Harvard College. Since Boston was only a few miles from Quincy, Louisa was able to see her children more often. In August 1807, she gave birth to a third son, Charles Francis.

In the Senate, John Quincy was engaged in a heated argument. British ships had been attacking American ships. Then they forced the sailors to serve aboard British vessels. Some senators wanted to pass an embargo. This would stop all shipping trade between the United States and Europe.

An embargo would hurt New England merchants, including many in Massachusetts. John Quincy, however, believed it was the right way to go. He voted "yes" on the Embargo Act of 1807. "This measure will cost you and me our seats," he remarked to another senator.

Sure enough, in May 1808, the Massachusetts legislature chose another man to replace John Quincy as senator. Bitterly, he resigned and went home to Boston.

The following year, President James Madison asked John Quincy to go to Russia as the U.S. minister. John Quincy did not have the nerve to tell Louisa she would have to leave their two older boys behind in Quincy. He had his brother, Thomas, tell her instead. Louisa was crushed at the thought of being thousands of miles away from her children. At least she could take the new baby.

In the early 1800s, the British were attacking American ships and forcing American sailors to serve on British ships. This practice was called impressment.

☆ ☆ ☆ ☆ ☆ ☆ ☆ ☆ ☆ ☆ ☆ ☆ ☆ ☆ ☆

CHAPTER FOUR

Life and Death in St. Petersburg

* * * * * * * * * * * * * * * * * *

After weeks of travel, the Adamses arrived in the glittering Russian capital of St. Petersburg. Wearing a silver hoop skirt and a crimson cloak, Louisa was presented to Czar Alexander. At once, she and John Quincy were swept into the city's swirling social life. Almost every night, there were court receptions, elegant dinners, and diplomatic balls. Parties often lasted until three or four o'clock in the morning.

John Quincy's salary was $9,000 a year—twice what he had received in the Netherlands. But the lifestyle of a diplomat in St. Petersburg was expensive. The French ambassador, for instance, kept sixty-five

* * * * * * * * * * * * * * * * * *

This snowy scene in St. Petersburg, Russia, shows St. Isaac's Cathedral in the background. Even today, the golden dome of this cathedral can be seen all over the city.

servants. He spent $350,000 a year on parties alone. John Quincy and Louisa could hardly make ends meet. For the first year, they rented rooms in a hotel where rats scurried across the floor.

In August 1811, Louisa gave birth to a beautiful baby girl. It was John Quincy's decision to name her Louisa Catherine. Louisa was thrilled with her new little daughter. When they went out for strolls, she looked on proudly while people admired the baby and tweaked her rosy cheeks.

The next spring, Louisa watched thousands of Russian troops march off to war. Napoleon Bonaparte of France had been conquering all of Europe. Now, in June 1812, his Grand Army of 500,000 men invaded Russia. News from the United States was alarming, too. The British were still kidnapping American sailors and forcing them to

Napoleon (1769–1821)

☆ ☆

He stood only five feet two inches (157 centimeters) tall, but the "Little Corporal," Emperor Napoleon I, conquered and ruled most of Europe for nearly sixteen years. Napoleon Bonaparte was born on the French island of Corsica on August 15, 1769, the second of eight children. Napoleon, clearly a military genius, moved to Paris, where he rose rapidly through the ranks of the French army. Between 1793 and 1815, Napoleon conquered most of Europe, crowning himself emperor in 1804. In France, he reorganized the government, simplified the

court system, and centralized control of the schools. Modern countries still use some of his systems and laws. Defeated by an allied army in 1814, Napoleon was exiled to the island of Elba. In March 1815, he escaped. As Louisa made her perilous journey from St. Petersburg, Napoleon was marching toward Paris with the very troops sent to capture him. He reigned again for only a hundred days, until his defeat at Waterloo. He lived out his days under close guard on the distant island of St. Helena, where he died in 1821.

Napoleon Bonaparte in 1813

Napoleon and his Grand Army of 500,000 men invaded Russia in June 1812.

work on British ships. Finally, the United States declared war on Great Britain. This was known as the War of 1812.

Meanwhile, baby Louisa had grown plump and healthy. But in the summer, she got sick and began wasting away. Louisa was frantic. No one knew what was wrong. One doctor suggested that Louisa take her to the country for some fresh air. But in a few days, the baby began having convulsions. Louisa rushed the infant back to St. Petersburg. On September 15, at the age of thirteen months, the baby died.

Louisa sank into a depression. Nothing she did could lift the pain of her loss. She wrote in her diary: "I read, I work, I endeavor to occupy myself usefully but it is all in vain." The gloomy Russian winter did not help Louisa's mood. Mid-winter sunlight lasted only a few hours. The temperature was often thirty or forty degrees below zero

Through the winter, John Quincy insisted that Louisa keep up the exhausting round of parties. In his mind, activity was a sure cure for the blues.

The War of 1812: Fast Facts

WHAT: "Second War of American Independence"

WHEN: 1812–1815

WHO: Between Britain and the United States

WHERE: Battles took place from Canada south to New Orleans, and as far west as the Great Lakes, with many important naval engagements

The Battle of Lake Erie, September 1813

WHY: Britain and France, who were at war with each other, were keeping the United States from trading freely, putting the new country's economy in danger. Other issues involved the British practices of impressing American sailors for British service and arming Native Americans in the Northwest Territory.

OUTCOME: Little was gained by either side, and there was much loss of life. However, the United States emerged with a new sense of nationhood and national pride.

Having Babies

✮ ✮

Families in the eighteenth century usually included many more children than they do today. Imagine being one of twenty-two children like Louisa's mother! More typically, families might number eight or ten children. Louisa had eight sisters and brothers. Such large families meant that women were generally pregnant or breast-feeding from the time they married in their early twenties until they became too old to have children, usually about twenty years later. Most women lost at least one baby before birth (called a miscarriage). Louisa herself lost eight of her twelve pregnancies. Such repeated sorrow was not at all uncommon in those days before modern medicine and care. To make matters worse, many children—like Louisa's daughter—died in infancy or childhood of diseases such as dysentery, whooping cough, and smallpox. Today, those diseases are preventable. Then, nearly half of all children died before the age of six. Babies were born at home, usually with the help of a midwife or a female relative and without pain medication. Obviously, eighteenth-century mothers led exhausting lives, and soon women began to have fewer children. By 1820, families usually included five or six children—still a houseful by modern standards! Today, on the average, American women have only one or two children.

Louisa noted that she had read fifty-three books that winter. One of them, *Treatises on Diseases of the Mind,* had been a gift from her husband.

Meanwhile, to deprive the French of supplies, Russians set fire to their own city of Moscow. As the harsh Russian winter descended, Napoleon's troops were dropping from hunger and fatigue. They began a sorrowful retreat. In one defeat after another, Napoleon saw his empire crumble. All of Europe was relieved in April 1814 when he gave up and went into exile.

In June 1814, John Quincy received a message from President James

John Quincy Adams and Britain's Lord Gambier shake hands after the signing of the Treaty of Ghent, which ended the War of 1812.

Madison. He was to go at once to the city of Ghent in Belgium. There, he was to begin working out a peace treaty with England. On Christmas Eve 1814, the Treaty of Ghent was signed, ending the War of 1812.

News traveled slowly in those days. General Andrew Jackson did not know that a peace treaty had been signed. On January 8, 1815, he massacred British troops in the Battle of New Orleans. Even though it was a useless battle, Jackson became a popular hero.

With his duties in Ghent completed, John Quincy went on to Paris.

General Andrew Jackson celebrated victory at the Battle of New Orleans on January 8, 1815, two weeks after the Treaty of Ghent had been signed.

To deprive the French of any supplies, the people of Moscow burned their city on September 14, 1812.

Napoleon's defeated troops, unable to withstand their hunger and fatigue, began their retreat from Russia in the winter of 1812.

From there, he wrote to Louisa. Get rid of the furniture, he instructed; pack up and close down all our affairs, bring little Charles, and come to Paris.

Louisa was astounded when she read the letter. She barely knew the Russian language. Yet, she had to wrap up six years' worth of life in Russia. For weeks, she packed, sold household goods, and said goodbye to friends.

On the last day, she hired a carriage, a team of horses, two coachmen, and a maid. On February 12, 1815—Louisa's fortieth birthday—she and seven-year-old Charles left St. Petersburg.

Huge snowdrifts covered the roads. The men put the carriage on runners so it coasted along like a sleigh. Before long, all their food and wine was

The Boulevard des Italiens in Paris as it looked about the time Louisa arrived after her frightening trip from St. Petersburg

frozen solid. On they drove, staying in filthy inns along the desolate route.

When the snows began to melt, they removed the runners and relied on wheels. Then the carriage kept sinking into the muddy, slushy ground. Time after time, they called upon peasants to pull them out of the mud. When they reached the Vistula River, its icy surface was beginning to thaw. Louisa sat frozen with terror as the carriage crossed the thinning ice.

One day, she found that Charles's silver cup had been stolen. Another time, all the money was stolen out of her purse. An innkeeper recognized one of Louisa's servants. He warned her that the man was "a desperate villain of the very worst character." She had no choice but to keep him, though.

New horrors faced Louisa as she crossed the Prussian frontier. The countryside was littered with the rotting bodies of soldiers killed in Napoleon's wars. Bones stuck up from the ground like stubble in a cornfield.

When they crossed into France, a rumor was going around that Napoleon was coming back. His old troops stormed through the countryside, ready for action. When they spied Louisa's Russian carriage, they were in the mood for an execution.

In the nick of time, an officer rode up. Louisa showed him her papers. "This is an American woman on her way to Paris to meet her husband," he shouted. "Let her pass."

At once, the mob backed off. "*Vive les Américains!*" they cried—Long live the Americans! "*Vive Napoléon!*" Louisa replied. For the rest of her trip, Louisa gained safe passage by shouting "*Vive Napoléon!*"

On March 20, Louisa stayed at an inn not far from Paris. That same day, Napoleon was marching triumphantly into the French capital. In the morning, the weary travelers were on the road again. Now, only the dreaded Forest of Bondy lay between Louisa and Paris. This was a hideout for bandits who lurked in the shadows and pounced upon unsuspecting travelers. Louisa mustered all her courage for this last frightful ordeal.

As the coach rumbled through the forest, Louisa began to notice a rider in the distance. He "appeared to be making a prodigious effort to overtake us." To her horror, her horses slowed down and the rider caught up to them.

"My imaginary highwayman came up very politely," she wrote, "and informed me that for the last half hour he had been apprehensive that the wheel of my carriage would come off."

What a relief! The party turned back, fixed the wheel, and took off again through the forest. On March 23, the rickety carriage arrived safely at the gates of Paris. At 11:00 P.M., Louisa and little Charles stepped out of the coach at John Quincy's hotel.

John Quincy was out at the theater but soon returned. Louisa reported that he was "perfectly astonished at

Napoleon escaped from exile on the island of Elba in 1815 and made a triumphant return to Paris on March 20, three days before Louisa arrived in the French capital from St. Petersburg.

my adventures, as everything in Paris was quiet, and it had never occurred to him that it would have been otherwise in any other part of the country." Maybe he had not noticed that Paris was in an uproar over Napoleon's return.

Many years later, Louisa wrote of her adventures in *Narrative of a Journey from Russia to France, 1815.*

She hoped her story would show that women were not as weak and helpless as people thought.

In May, John Quincy was appointed U.S. minister to Great Britain. At once, he sent for sons George and John. The Adamses rented a house near London and called it Little Boston. For the first time in almost twenty years, Louisa enjoyed a peace-

Louisa, John Quincy, and their three sons arrived in New York Harbor in August 1817, after a fifty-three-day ocean voyage during which Louisa had yet another miscarriage.

ful, happy family life. However, it did not last very long. James Monroe, who had become the fifth U.S. president in 1816, wrote to John Quincy asking him to be his secretary of state.

In June 1817, Louisa, John Quincy, and their three boys set sail for New York. Louisa, pregnant again, must have dreaded the grueling trip. During the fifty-three-day ocean voyage, she suffered another miscarriage. It would be her last.

In August, the family sailed into New York Harbor. They had been away for eight years. This time, they were home to stay.

CHAPTER FIVE

Social Calls and Campaign Balls

* * * * * * * * * * * * * * * * * * *

The old house in Quincy was swarming with relatives. Cousins, nieces, and nephews had come from miles around to welcome the Adamses back. Louisa relaxed, took long walks, and went fishing with her boys. She especially loved spending time with Abigail. Finally, it seemed that Louisa and Abigail were becoming warm friends.

"She herself told me she was sorry she had not better understood my character," Louisa wrote in her diary.

Soon, Louisa and John Quincy were off to Washington. All three boys were left to attend school in Boston. Louisa was sad to leave her children again.

* * * * * * * * * * * * * * * * * * *

The Adams house in Quincy was full of relatives when the young Adams family arrived from London before John Quincy took up his post as secretary of state.

The three sons of Louisa and John Quincy attended Boston Latin School while their parents were in Washington, D.C.

State of the Secretary of State

✫ ✫ ✫ ✫ ✫ ✫ ✫ ✫ ✫ ✫ ✫ ✫ ✫ ✫ ✫ ✫ ✫ ✫ ✫ ✫

When President George Washington selected the first cabinet in 1789, it included only the secretaries of war, state, and treasury. He named Thomas Jefferson the first secretary of state. Much like that of today's secretary of state, Jefferson's job included dealing with foreign governments and keeping track of world affairs. When Jefferson took up the position, he had five clerks on his staff and two diplomats abroad. Only four foreign countries sent representatives to the United States. It was not until 1909 that the office established geographical divisions headed by specialists. Now, the secretary of state is the highest-ranking member of the president's cabinet, which has grown from Washington's original three departments to fourteen. Madeleine Albright became the first woman secretary of state under President Bill Clinton. She headed up a staff larger than the local government of a medium-sized city, with diplomatic posts in 180 of the world's 190 countries. By the way, only six secretaries of state have gone on to become president, although many others have tried and failed to be elected.

But she knew that Boston's Latin School would give the boys a good preparation for Harvard.

As secretary of state, John Quincy was a member of the president's cabinet, or group of close advisers. As a "cabinet wife," Louisa, too, had clear duties. She was to pay official visits to other Washington wives. A wife's visit showed that her husband respected the other's husband.

To John Quincy, Louisa's visits were more than just politeness. Presidents Jefferson, Madison, and Monroe had all served as secretary of state. John Quincy sensed that he, too, would move on to be president some day. No one could help him more than Louisa.

"It is understood," Louisa wrote in her diary, "that a man who is ambitious to become President of the

John Quincy Adams

Thomas Jefferson

James Madison

James Monroe

Elizabeth Monroe, wife of President James Monroe

United States must make his wife visit the Ladies of the members of Congress first. Otherwise, he is totally inefficient to fill so high an office."

Every morning before work, John Quincy wrote out Louisa's calling cards for the day. She was to present her card at each home she visited. Some days there were as many as twenty-five homes on her list. Even if no one was home, leaving the card would show that she had been there.

Soon people began to complain. The secretary of state's wife returned visits, but she never made the *first* call. Insulted couples decided to get even. When Louisa threw a big party, only three people came.

The ladies' visits were such a big issue that the Senate met to discuss them. Then Mrs. Monroe, the president's wife, summoned John Quincy for a meeting. Next, the president himself called him in to talk about the visits. A few days later, the entire cabinet met on the subject. John Quincy wrote furious letters to the president and vice president. All of Washington joined in the fuss. Finally, with John Quincy's blessing, Louisa put her foot down. She would return all visits, but she would not make the first call.

Even a century later, the battle over the visits raged on. In 1921, Lou Hoover, wife of Secretary of Commerce Herbert Hoover, led a revolt about the "leaving of cards." Cabinet wives finally announced that they would no longer make official calls.

In 1921, to the relief of many Washington wives, Lou Hoover, wife of Secretary of Commerce Herbert Hoover, convinced cabinet wives to declare that they would no longer make official calls.

Giving parties was another way Louisa could campaign for her husband. Every Tuesday evening was "open house" at the Adams home. John Quincy was not the social type. While he grumbled, Louisa organized the Tuesday events. Congressmen and their wives enjoyed lavish outlays of food. Louisa played the piano and the harp and sang. The Adams parties became so popular that even John Quincy was amazed.

Why was it so important to please the members of Congress? Today, political parties hold conventions every four years. Representatives at

Louisa played the harp at her Tuesday evening open houses for congressmen and their wives.

The Adamses' grand ball in honor of Andrew Jackson (center) was a spectacular success.

the conventions pick the candidates who will run for president. But political conventions did not begin until the 1830s. In the Adamses' time, Congress chose the candidates.

In December 1823, John Quincy thought of another way to boost his chances for president. They would put on a grand ball, he told Louisa. It would be in honor of Andrew Jackson, hero of the Battle of New Orleans. The date would be January 8, the anniversary of the battle.

This must have seemed an odd idea to Louisa. After all, nine years had passed since the battle—and Andrew Jackson himself was planning to run for president. "I objected much to the plan," she wrote, "but was overpowered by John's arguments and the thing was settled." With less than three weeks to prepare, Louisa snapped into action.

Servants, nieces, and nephews were put to work. Some made wreaths and garlands to hang. Others polished serving dishes and silverware. Furniture was pushed aside and beds rolled up to make way for the crowd. Louisa even had new pillars built in the parlor to support the weight of people on the floor above.

On the big evening, guests began to arrive at 7:30. Louisa, posted by the door, watched for the guest of honor. At 9:00, Jackson's carriage pulled up. Louisa took his arm and led him through the admiring crowd. Women stood on chairs to catch a glimpse of the popular general. Jackson toasted Louisa, ate some food, then left for another party.

At one point, an oil lamp fell off the wall and landed on Louisa's head. Hot oil ran down her shoulders and ruined her dress. Always the perfect hostess, Louisa made a joke of it, ran and changed her dress, and quickly reappeared. To Louisa's delight, the ball was a spectacular success. It was the talk of the town for months.

By election time, several candidates had stepped forward. Adams and Jackson were the favorites. Nasty news stories and cartoons appeared on both sides. Some said that Jackson's wife, Rachel, was old, fat, and smoked a corncob pipe. Others said that Louisa was European-bred and too fancy for America.

Rachel and Andrew Jackson

★ ★

Even though Andrew Jackson finally won the presidency in 1828, his wife Rachel did not live to become First Lady. The Jacksons had been happily married for more than thirty years at the time of her death in 1828, but unfortunate circumstances surrounded their early relationship. Rachel thought herself to be legally divorced from her first husband by the time she and Jackson wed in 1791. They did not realize, however, that her divorce was not final. In 1794, they were forced to marry again. For the rest of their lives together, political enemies attacked the Jacksons for this episode in their past. Nonetheless, Andrew and Rachel, both raised on the rugged frontier, enjoyed a happy and companionable marriage, raising two nephews of Rachel's along the way. During the 1828 presidential campaign, John Quincy Adams's supporters heaped so much insult on Rachel that Andrew Jackson blamed them for her death three months before his inauguration.

In November 1824, voters across the country went to the polls. They voted for electors, who would then cast ballots for president. To win, a candidate needed 131 electoral votes.

When the votes were counted, Jackson had received 99 electoral votes, and John Quincy got 84. Since no one had enough votes to win, the House of Representatives was required to vote. On February 9, 1825, the congressmen chose John Quincy Adams as sixth president of the United States.

☆ ☆ ☆ ☆ ☆ ☆ ☆ ☆ ☆ ☆ ☆ ☆ ☆ ☆ ☆

CHAPTER SIX

Dreary Days in the White House

★ ★ ★ ★ ★ ★ ★ ★ ★ ★ ★ ★ ★ ★ ★ ★ ★

On March 4, 1825, John Quincy took his oath of office as president. In April, he and Louisa moved into the President's Mansion. By now, people were beginning to call it the White House.

During the campaign, Louisa had said that John Quincy's election would "put me in a prison." Now, as she looked around her new home, she must have felt gloomy indeed.

British forces had burned the White House in the War of 1812, and it was still being rebuilt. No shade trees stood on the grounds—only a few sheds for horses and cows. There was no indoor plumbing and no

★ ★ ★ ★ ★ ★ ★ ★ ★ ★ ★ ★ ★ ★ ★ ★ ★

The south side of the White House as it looked about the time Louisa and John Quincy Adams lived there as President and First Lady

running water. President Monroe had removed his furniture from the White House, so most of the rooms were bare.

"There is something in this great unsocial house," Louisa wrote, "which depresses my spirits beyond expression and makes it impossible for me to feel at home or to fancy that I have a home anywhere."

Louisa was worn out from the campaign. Over the years, she had grown weak and thin. The air inside the White House was bad for her health, too. At that time, people burned anthracite coal to keep warm. Fumes

President John Quincy Adams swam in the Potomac River each morning before he joined Louisa for a late breakfast in the White House.

from the coal caused lung problems. During the winter months, Louisa often stayed in her bedroom for days at a time.

The Adamses lived quietly in the White House. John Quincy rose early and went swimming in the Potomac River. At ten, they had breakfast while reading the newspapers. In the old days—in St. Petersburg and Berlin—evenings had been filled with a whirlwind of parties. Now, however, they rarely went out at night. Dinner was at five. Then they read books until bedtime at eleven.

Louisa filled her dreary days with

writing. Letters, memoirs, poems, and plays flowed from her pen daily. In the summer of 1825, at the age of fifty, Louisa began writing *Record of a Life, or My Story*.

Actually, Louisa had no idea what her role as First Lady was. In 1789, when George Washington became the first president, people wondered what to call him. Some suggested "His Highness" or "His Excellency." They were still used to having kings and queens. George's wife, Martha, was called "Lady Washington."

Dolley Madison, the fourth First Lady, had been famous as a hostess. Because she took part in the president's decisions, some people called her "Presidentress." Elizabeth Monroe, the fifth president's wife, shied away from parties. Yet she ordered her expensive gowns from France. Her nickname was "Queen Elizabeth." Louisa, like Dolley and Elizabeth, had visited the royal courts of Europe. But she did not play the part of a glamorous, fashionable lady.

After Louisa's time, Americans valued humble beginnings. If a president and his wife had been born

One of the gowns worn by Louisa when she was First Lady

Women's Changing Lives

The lives of Louisa Adams and her mother-in-law Abigail represent the changing experiences of early American women. Abigail, like other women of her generation, was toughened by colonial life and liberated by the Revolution. She became a skilled "farmeress" in Massachusetts during her husband's long absences, for which he praised her lavishly. She enjoyed in her marriage a certain partnership, even though laws and social customs limited her rights to own property or acquire an education. Abigail began to see possibilities for herself and other women that she expressed in a letter to John in 1776 as he worked to form the new American government: "In the new Code of Laws which I suppose it will be necessary for you to make I desire you would Remember the Ladies . . . "

Unfortunately for Louisa's generation, however, who came of age after the Revolution, such sentiments remained largely ignored. Throughout Louisa's lifetime, women's roles became even more centered in the home. New attitudes toward children began to stress the quality of child rearing. Birthrates fell as women increased their attention to individual children and as their roles as mothers intensified. Even the nature of marriage changed. Where once unions were arranged by parents based on matters of practicality, men and women now began to marry for love. This new romantic attitude may have elevated women to a pedestal, but it did little for their equality or education, as John Quincy indicated when he remarked that in women, mental abilities seemed unbecoming. For women of Louisa's generation who wished to experience the fullness of life, it must have been a very difficult time.

in log cabins, they were more attractive. Louisa did not fit this mold, either. She was no homespun frontier woman. Actually, Louisa was the country's only First Lady to have been born outside the United States. So it is not surprising that she simply fell through the cracks between two trends in American history.

In 1826, as the Fourth of July approached, the nation prepared for its own birthday celebration. It would be the fiftieth anniversary of the Declaration of Independence. At the same time, two old men lay on their deathbeds: ninety-year-old John Adams and eighty-three-year-old Thomas Jefferson. On July 4, within hours of each other, both men died.

Louisa had loved her kindly father-in-law. "The Ex-President John Adams never said an unkind word to me," she wrote in her diary, "but even to the hour of his death, treated me with the utmost tenderness."

As president, John Quincy was not able to accomplish all he would have liked. He knew he had not been elected by the people but by a vote in Congress. After 1826, Andrew Jackson's supporters outnumbered John Quincy's in Congress. He began to feel rejected and powerless.

The Adamses' son George was a constant concern. George was more like his mother than his father. He enjoyed art, poetry, theater, and novels. Schoolwork was not his strong point.

Still, John Quincy pushed George to attend Harvard and become a lawyer. That would prepare him for a life of public service. John Quincy expected George, as the oldest son, to follow in the footsteps of his father and grandfather.

George obeyed, but he had a hard time. On the day of his Harvard entrance exam, he threw up. John had no patience for George's "laziness." His letters were full of orders. Discipline! Duty! Rise early! Make lists! Study the classics! John Quincy was probably echoing the words of his own parents. But the letters must have struck George like a pack of barking dogs.

Several times, Louisa left the White House and rushed to visit George in Boston. She found his rent-

George Washington Adams, the oldest son of Louisa and John Quincy

John Adams (1735–1826) and Thomas Jefferson (1743–1826)

⭐ ⭐ ⭐ ⭐ ⭐ ⭐ ⭐ ⭐ ⭐ ⭐ ⭐ ⭐ ⭐ ⭐ ⭐ ⭐ ⭐ ⭐ ⭐ ⭐

The lives and work of these two statesmen reflect the early years of the American democracy. Jefferson, author of the Declaration of Independence, praised Adams for his support of the cause. But as the nation grew, they disagreed about the distribution of authority. Adams, as second president, believed in a strong federal

John Adams

government. Jefferson, the third president, promoted the rights of individual states. As the years went by, they put aside their differences and began a remarkable correspondence about the issues of the day. Both men died on July 4, 1826, the fiftieth anniversary of the signing of the Declaration of Independence. Unaware that Jefferson had died several hours before, Adams's last words were "Thomas Jefferson still lives."

Thomas Jefferson

Harvard: An Adams Family Tradition

✦ ✦

Through the years, most Adams men, including John Quincy, attended and taught at Harvard in Cambridge, Massachusetts. John Quincy's son Charles even turned down the presidency of the college. Today, several dormitories are named after the family. This makes sense, since both the Adamses and the school trace their roots to the country's beginnings. Harvard was the first college in America. Founded by the Puritans of the Massachusetts Bay Colony in 1636 to teach ministers, the college was named after its first supporter, clergyman John Harvard. From its first class of only twelve students, Harvard now enrolls more than 16,000 and is among the finest schools in the world. The university's reputation is grounded in nearly four centuries of academic excellence, especially in preparing students for national public service. To the present day, more presidents have been educated at Harvard than at any other institution.

Harvard College

ed rooms dark and messy. Even worse, though, was George's state of mind. He was so depressed he could hardly leave his room. He saw and heard things that didn't exist. His mood changed from one moment to the next.

As the 1828 presidential election drew near, John Quincy knew he had no chance to win the presidency. As expected, Andrew Jackson won the election.

In March 1829, Louisa and John Quincy packed up and left the White House. As their carriage rolled away from the great mansion, Louisa looked forward to peace and quiet.

CHAPTER SEVEN

Making a Mark of Her Own

★ ★ ★ ★ ★ ★ ★ ★ ★ ★ ★ ★ ★ ★ ★ ★

The Adamses hoped to settle back into the old house in Quincy. Meanwhile, they rented a comfortable farmhouse in Meridian Hill, not far from the White House. They invited George to spend the summer with them. As an extra attraction, Louisa promised to keep John Quincy quiet.

On May 2, 1829, a carriage came rumbling up the road to Meridian Hill. If Louisa expected to see George, she soon had a cruel surprise. It was a friend bringing the morning's newspaper. An article said that George Washington Adams had taken a boat trip and had been lost overboard. His body had not yet been

★ ★ ★ ★ ★ ★ ★ ★ ★ ★ ★ ★ ★ ★ ★ ★

Charles Francis Adams

John Adams II

80

After serving in the highest office in the land, what does a president do next? Few of this country's chief executives have chosen to retire. Education seems to be a natural second act for presidents. Among the early founders of the democracy, former presidents Thomas Jefferson, James Madison, and James Monroe went about supplying its most needed resource—educated citizens. Jefferson founded and served as rector of the University of Virginia. Madison and Monroe served on the board of regents. Yale, Stanford, Princeton, Emory, the University of Buffalo, and Rutgers University all employed presidential professors. Many presidents continued their lives in public service. John Quincy Adams and Andrew Johnson served in Congress. In 1861, John Tyler was elected to the Congress of the Confederacy, formed to govern the South just before the Civil War. William Howard Taft was appointed chief justice of the Supreme Court. Writing, farming, traveling, and charity work has occupied many former president's hours as well. In recent times, former President Jimmy Carter helped to negotiate peace in Bosnia and serves the American poor by building houses through Habitat for Humanity.

found. Was it an accident, or did George commit suicide? No one knew.

Louisa and John Quincy were devastated. In their grief and pain, they drew closer. Both parents blamed themselves for the tragedy. John Quincy began to see that he might have been too harsh with George. Louisa blamed herself for not recognizing how sick her son was really was.

Still, they had two living sons. Charles, the youngest, was building his career as a lawyer. The middle son, John, had married Louisa's niece Mary. Their first baby, Mary Louisa, had just been born in the White House. John Quincy put young John in charge of a grain mill he owned in Washington, D.C.

The Adamses returned to Quincy

and settled into a comfortable routine. Louisa enjoyed playing the piano and fishing, while John Quincy tended his garden and fruit trees. In the summer of 1830, local citizens urged John Quincy to run as their congressman. He won by a landslide. John Quincy was eager to be in public life again, but

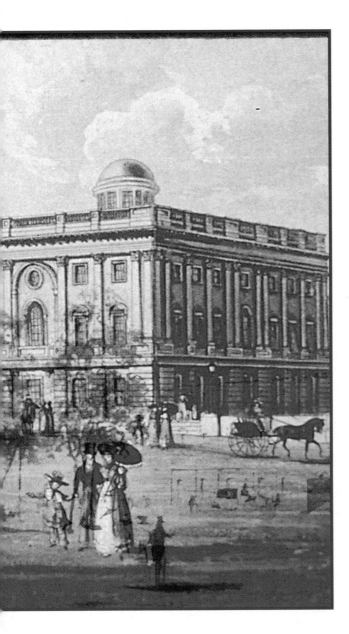

The Capitol about 1830, when John Quincy Adams returned to Washington, D.C., as a congressman

looked at her life. She had been a loving mother and a proper homemaker. She had been the dutiful wife of a diplomat, a senator, a secretary of state, and a U.S. president. Now, she wondered, who was *she?* Where could she make her *own* mark in the world?

Louisa had been thinking deeply about slavery. "The awful question of Slavery is before the publick," she wrote, "and the question is of so fearfully exciting a nature it keeps me in a state of perpetual alarm."

To Louisa, it was a moral question. Clearly, she believed, slavery was against the laws of God. After all, God had led his people out of slavery in Egypt. To sort out her thoughts, she wrote pages and pages of anti-slavery arguments in her journal.

Louisa was inspired by abolitionist Sarah Grimké. Sarah traveled throughout New England giving fiery

Louisa was just as glad to be away from it. At first, she refused to go to Washington, but she finally gave in.

At this point, Louisa sat back and

The Grimké Sisters

Sarah (1792–1873) and Angelina (1805–1879) Grimké came from a prominent South Carolina family. Brought up as Southern belles to attend balls and parties, both rebelled against the brutal treatment they saw their servants endure. They moved to the North and joined other abolitionists. The American Anti-Slavery Society asked Angelina to hold meetings for New York women interested in the cause. Sarah used the pen as her weapon, writing a pamphlet to ministers in the South, persuading them with arguments from the Bible to give up slavery. Angelina's lectures, filled with details of the suffering she had witnessed among slaves, drew larger and larger crowds of both women and men. This created a great controversy because women were not supposed to speak to "mixed" audiences. But public disapproval only inspired the busy Grimké sisters to fight a new battle. Their publications are among America's first to argue for women's rights.

Sarah Grimké

speeches against slavery. The two women began a long letter-writing relationship.

Sarah and Louisa were also inflamed about women's rights. Both felt that women should be able to vote. For Louisa, slavery and women's rights were similar. She believed that God had created all people as equals—men and women, black and white. Sarah encouraged Louisa's thinking. Without equal rights, she said, women were only "white slaves of the North."

In the midst of this, another tragedy struck the Adamses. Their son John, eager to make his father's grain mill a success, was working from before dawn until late at night. The damp air around the riverside mill began to damage his joints. He often had severe fevers, too. John became deeply depressed and drank too much, but he kept working all the same. In 1834, he became so sick that he died.

Now entering their later years, Louisa and John Quincy had only one child left. More than ever before, they looked to their grandchildren for comfort and joy.

In Congress, John Quincy was consumed with the issue of slavery. Hundreds of abolitionists sent anti-slavery petitions to him. Louisa spent hours counting them and writing out copies. Day after day, John Quincy presented the petitions in Congress.

In 1836, a group of Southern congressmen managed to pass a "gag rule." It said that no more anti-slavery petitions would be heard in the House of Representatives. For the next eight years, John Quincy fought to overturn the ruling. At last, in 1844, it was repealed.

With few public duties, Louisa was enjoying the chance to develop her mind. She studied history books and often listened to debates in the Capitol. Louisa wished that she—and all women—were better educated. At the time, people didn't think it was proper for girls to learn much. They believed that education made a woman unladylike.

In 1840, at the age of sixty-five, Louisa began writing her autobiography. She called it *The Adventures of a Nobody*. Poor Louisa still felt like a nobody. Looking over her life, she

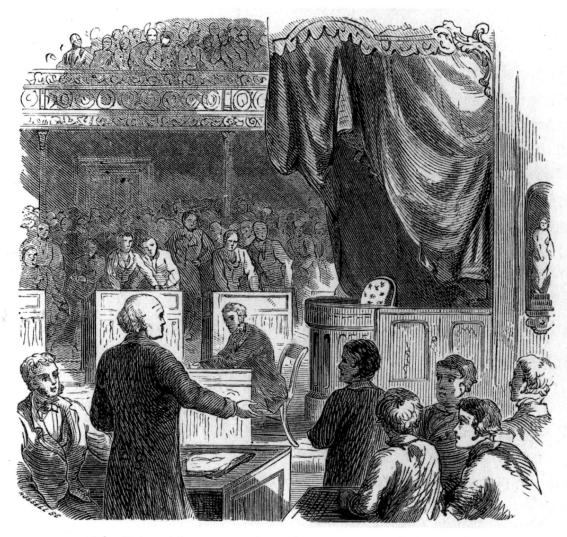

As a congressman, John Quincy Adams presented anti-slavery petitions in the House of Representatives until a group of Southern congressmen passed a gag rule.

thought she had done nothing of any account. If only there were some small way she could make a difference!

In 1846, Louisa hired a cook named Julia, a slave who belonged to a friend. For years, Julia had been saving money to buy her freedom. The price was $400—the amount she would bring if she were sold at a slave auction.

Louisa liked Julia. In the summer, she wanted to take her along to

The Amistad Incident

★ ★

John Quincy Adams was not known as an abolitionist. Yet, when asked to represent the African captives of the Spanish slave ship *Amistad* before the Supreme Court in 1841, the former president knew he had to take the case. Kidnapped or sold into slavery from their African villages, fifty-four men, women, and children were shipped to the Caribbean. During their journey, they revolted, killing the captain and the cook. Attempting to sail back to Africa, the thirty-nine surviving slaves were captured by the American ship *Washington* and jailed on American soil. The Spanish government demanded that the *Amistad* and its cargo be returned to Spain, where the captives would be punished for murder. Spain, however, was breaking the law. Although slave owning remained legal, the slave trade was not. When John Quincy Adams defended the captive Africans before the Supreme Court, he relied on the Declaration of Independence to convince the justices that the Africans be treated not as property or murderers but as victims who deserved their freedom. Adams achieved his goal. The Supreme Court freed the captives and struck slavery a severe blow. Today, the *Amistad* incident is recalled in books, a movie, and even an opera called *Amistad*.

The death of Captain Ferrer on board the Amistad, July 1839

John Quincy Adams defended the right of petition in Congress for eight years. The gag order against anti-slavery petitions was finally overturned in 1844.

Quincy. However, Washington was considered part of the South, while Quincy was in a Northern state. It was against the law to take a slave from the South to the North. To guard against the slave escaping, a person had to post a bond. That is, they had to give the owner the slave's full price before leaving.

Louisa could not afford the bond, so she left without Julia. She worried about her kindly cook, though. What if some heartless slaveholder bought Julia, she wondered. It was well known that some slave owners treated their slaves with unspeakable cruelty.

On returning to Washington, Louisa studied Julia's situation. By herself, Julia had saved $275. Only another $125 stood between Julia and her freedom. By this time, Louisa had a small income of her very own, which her brother had left to her. She quietly paid the remaining amount and set Julia free.

This simple act meant a lot to Louisa. She once wrote that if she could free Julia, "I should be almost as glad as if I was buying my own freedom."

☆ ☆ ☆ ☆ ☆ ☆ ☆ ☆ ☆ ☆ ☆ ☆ ☆ ☆ ☆

CHAPTER EIGHT

"A Vision of Silver Gray"

John Quincy's constant fighting in Congress was hard on him. Louisa worried about him all the time. Over and over, she cried out her distress in her diary: "The extreme uneasiness I feel at the state of Mr. Adams's health is beyond language to express!"

Louisa was annoyed that John Quincy would not take care of himself. He still took swims in the icy Potomac River. Even in winter, he insisted on sleeping with the windows open. Sometimes he forgot to change his shirt. When Louisa pointed this out, John Quincy was irritated.

In November 1846, John Quincy was strolling down

John Quincy Adams collapsed at his desk on February 21, 1848, and died two days later.

a street in Boston. All of a sudden, he had a stroke and fell to the ground. For months, he stayed in bed while Louisa cared for him. Soon, he was back in his old seat in Congress.

On February 21, 1848, John Quincy suddenly collapsed at his desk in the House of Representatives. Other congressmen placed him on a sofa and carried him into the Speaker's chamber. Louisa rushed to his side and spent a restless night in the Capitol. There, he remained in a coma until February 23, when he died.

After John Quincy's death, Louisa lived quietly in Washington. She redecorated the parlor of her home where, many years before, she had held the grand ball for General Jackson. On New Year's Day 1849, she gave one more big party. Two hundred guests paid their respects to the beloved lady.

That spring, Louisa suffered a stroke. For a while, her right hand and arm did not work. She was losing her sight and hearing, too, and could walk only with a cane.

Louisa asked her relatives not to try to entertain her. She wrote to her son Charles that "old persons best understand what suits them." It suited Louisa to read, write poetry, and take carriage rides in the countryside.

In early 1852, she had another stroke. This time, she could no longer leave her bed. Sisters, nieces, and daughters-in-law cared for her and hovered at her bedside. At noon on

May 15, 1852, seventy-seven-year-old Louisa died.

On the day of her funeral, Congress closed for a day of silence. Louisa was the first woman to be honored in this way. President Millard Fillmore, his cabinet, and dozens of congressmen attended the service.

One sad mourner was Louisa's fourteen-year-old grandson, Henry Adams. When Henry grew up, he wrote a history of the Adams family.

Henry Adams, Louisa's grandson

Charles Francis Adams (1807–1886)

☆ ☆

The famous Adams family dynasty did not stop with John Quincy and Louisa. Their only surviving child, Charles Francis, went on to a distinguished career as a politician, a diplomat, a historian, and editor of his father's diaries. He married the lively Abby Brooks in 1829. (Louisa had once warned her that Adams men were difficult in their dealings with women.) His most notable accomplishment came during the Civil War when he served as minister to Great Britain. Because they needed Southern cotton, the British threatened to recognize the independence of the Confederate states. Such a stand would have meant the end of the Union. Charles, a wise and well-liked statesman, persuaded them against it. Of Charles's seven children, four sons went on to gain fame as writers and historians.

This statue of Abigail Adams with her son John Quincy (left) and a memorial to John Quincy and Louisa (right) can both be seen at the United First Parish Church in Quincy, where Louisa and John Quincy are buried in the Adams family crypt.

Louisa, he said, "seemed a fragile creature to a boy who . . . took a distinct pleasure in looking at her delicate face." He remembered his grandmother as charming, with a "gentle voice and manner," and "singularly peaceful, a vision of silver gray."

Charles took his mother's body back to Quincy. There, she was laid to rest in the Adams family crypt beneath the United First Parish Church. Beside her lie John Quincy and her in-laws, Abigail and John. Today, visitors to the church can read these words outside her tomb:

Louisa Catherine Adams
Frail of Body, Simple in Tastes, and
   Retiring in Nature
She Filled the Onerous Positions To
   Which It Pleased God
To Assign Her With Grace, Dignity,
   and Fortitude

Portrait of America, 1852: Antebellum Days

✫ ✫

A girl born in 1852, the year Louisa Adams died, was expected to live only forty years or so. By that measure, Louisa herself lived a long life, passing at age seventy-seven. She survived many of the hazards of her day: illnesses for which doctors had no cure, miscarriages, and dangerous travels over land and sea. However, Louisa and other Americans in 1852 accepted the uncertainty of life and worked hard to expand the nation and prosper.

Today, we describe this period before the Civil War as *antebellum* (a Latin word meaning "before war"). By then, twenty million new Americans had swelled the population since 1775, and thirty-one states made up the Union. Immigrants, especially Germans escaping unrest in Europe, arrived in growing numbers. Pioneers settled beyond the Mississippi River and pushed relentlessly through the treacherous western wilderness to reach the newly discovered goldfields of California. On farms, where most Americans still lived, new mechanical reapers and plows made the work easier. In cities, industries thrived on making these new tools. A man named Elisha Otis invented a safe passenger elevator that would eventually enable city buildings to scrape the sky.

However, while antebellum America offered many opportunities, slavery cast its dark shadow over all. Divisions between North and South over the issue of slavery were growing wider. People and politicians argued: As the nation expanded, would new states join the Union as free or slave states? What should be done with runaway slaves? Should slavery be abolished? One of the most important events in 1852 was the publication of a book by Harriet Beecher Stowe called *Uncle Tom's Cabin*. Stowe believed strongly in freedom for the slaves and hoped that her book about the evils of slavery would unite the country against it. In the end, *Uncle Tom's Cabin* did much to push the nation toward war.

As the Civil War loomed, it was not at all clear in 1852 whether America, born the same year as Louisa, would outlive her by much.

The Presidents and Their First Ladies

YEARS IN OFFICE			
President	*Birth–Death*	*First Lady*	*Birth–Death*
1789–1797			
George Washington	1732–1799	Martha Dandridge Custis Washington	1731–1802
1797–1801			
John Adams	1735–1826	Abigail Smith Adams	1744–1818
1801–1809			
Thomas Jefferson†	1743–1826		
1809–1817			
James Madison	1751–1836	Dolley Payne Todd Madison	1768–1849
1817–1825			
James Monroe	1758–1831	Elizabeth Kortright Monroe	1768–1830
1825–1829			
John Quincy Adams	1767–1848	Louisa Catherine Johnson Adams	1775–1852
1829–1837			
Andrew Jackson†	1767–1845		
1837–1841			
Martin Van Buren†	1782–1862		
1841			
William Henry Harrison‡	1773–1841		
1841–1845			
John Tyler	1790–1862	Letitia Christian Tyler (1841–1842)	1790–1842
		Julia Gardiner Tyler (1844–1845)	1820–1889
1845–1849			
James K. Polk	1795–1849	Sarah Childress Polk	1803–1891
1849–1850			
Zachary Taylor	1784–1850	Margaret Mackall Smith Taylor	1788–1852
1850–1853			
Millard Fillmore	1800–1874	Abigail Powers Fillmore	1798–1853
1853–1857			
Franklin Pierce	1804–1869	Jane Means Appleton Pierce	1806–1863
1857–1861			
James Buchanan*	1791–1868		
1861–1865			
Abraham Lincoln	1809–1865	Mary Todd Lincoln	1818–1882
1865–1869			
Andrew Johnson	1808–1875	Eliza McCardle Johnson	1810–1876
1869–1877			
Ulysses S. Grant	1822–1885	Julia Dent Grant	1826–1902
1877–1881			
Rutherford B. Hayes	1822–1893	Lucy Ware Webb Hayes	1831–1889
1881			
James A. Garfield	1831–1881	Lucretia Rudolph Garfield	1832–1918
1881–1885			
Chester A. Arthur†	1829–1886		

† wife died before he took office   ‡ wife too ill to accompany him to Washington   * never married

1885–1889			
Grover Cleveland	1837–1908	Frances Folsom Cleveland	1864–1947
1889–1893			
Benjamin Harrison	1833–1901	Caroline Lavinia Scott Harrison	1832–1892
1893–1897			
Grover Cleveland	1837–1908	Frances Folsom Cleveland	1864–1947
1897–1901			
William McKinley	1843–1901	Ida Saxton McKinley	1847–1907
1901–1909			
Theodore Roosevelt	1858–1919	Edith Kermit Carow Roosevelt	1861–1948
1909–1913			
William Howard Taft	1857–1930	Helen Herron Taft	1861–1943
1913–1921			
Woodrow Wilson	1856–1924	Ellen Louise Axson Wilson (1913–1914)	1860–1914
		Edith Bolling Galt Wilson (1915–1921)	1872–1961
1921–1923			
Warren G. Harding	1865–1923	Florence Kling Harding	1860–1924
1923–1929			
Calvin Coolidge	1872–1933	Grace Anna Goodhue Coolidge	1879–1957
1929–1933			
Herbert Hoover	1874–1964	Lou Henry Hoover	1874–1944
1933–1945			
Franklin D. Roosevelt	1882–1945	Anna Eleanor Roosevelt	1884–1962
1945–1953			
Harry S. Truman	1884–1972	Bess Wallace Truman	1885–1982
1953–1961			
Dwight D. Eisenhower	1890–1969	Mamie Geneva Doud Eisenhower	1896–1979
1961–1963			
John F. Kennedy	1917–1963	Jacqueline Bouvier Kennedy	1929–1994
1963–1969			
Lyndon B. Johnson	1908–1973	Claudia Taylor (Lady Bird) Johnson	1912–
1969–1974			
Richard Nixon	1913–1994	Patricia Ryan Nixon	1912–1993
1974–1977			
Gerald Ford	1913–	Elizabeth Bloomer Ford	1918–
1977–1981			
James Carter	1924–	Rosalynn Smith Carter	1927–
1981–1989			
Ronald Reagan	1911–	Nancy Davis Reagan	1923–
1989–1993			
George Bush	1924–	Barbara Pierce Bush	1925–
1993–			
William Jefferson Clinton	1946–	Hillary Rodham Clinton	1947–

Louisa Catherine Johnson Adams Timeline

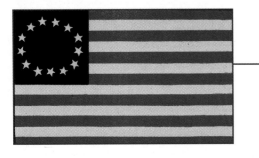

1775 ★ Louisa Catherine Johnson is born on February 12 in London, England

First shots of the Revolutionary War are fired at Lexington and Concord in Massachusetts

1776 ★ Declaration of Independence is signed

1777 ★ Congress authorizes the Stars and Stripes as the American flag

1778 ★ Louisa Catherine Johnson's family moves to Nantes, France

1781 ★ Articles of Confederation are ratified as a framework for governing the United States

British surrender at Yorktown

1783 ★ Treaty of Paris ends the Revolutionary War, and Great Britain recognizes the independence of the United States

Louisa Johnson's family moves back to London

1788 ★ U.S. Constitution is ratified by a majority of states

1789 ★ George Washington is inaugurated as president

French Revolution begins

1790 ★ Washington, D.C., is founded

1791 ★ Bill of Rights is ratified

1792 ★ George Washington is reelected president

1793 ★ King and queen of France are executed

Eli Whitney invents the cotton gin

1796 ★ John Adams is elected president

1797 ★ Louisa Johnson marries John Quincy Adams

John Quincy Adams is named U.S. minister to Prussia, and the Adamses move to Berlin

1800	★	Thomas Jefferson is elected president
1801	★	Louisa Adams's son, George Washington Adams, is born
		Louisa Adams comes to the United States for the first time, and the Adamses live in Quincy, Massachusetts
1803	★	United States purchases Louisiana Territory from France
		Louisa Adams's son, John Adams, is born
		John Quincy Adams is appointed U.S. senator from Massachusetts, and the Adamses move to Washington, D.C.
1804	★	Lewis and Clark expedition begins
		Thomas Jefferson is reelected president
		Napoleon crowns himself emperor of France
1806	★	Prussia is conquered by Napoleon's forces
1807	★	British navy impresses American seaman
		Louisa Adams's son, Charles Francis Adams, is born
1808	★	James Madison is elected president
		The Adamses move to Boston
1809	★	John Quincy Adams is named U.S. minister to Russia, and the Adamses move to St. Petersburg
1811	★	Louisa Adams's daughter Louisa Catherine Adams is born
1812	★	United States declares war on Great Britain, which begins the War of 1812
		James Madison is reelected president
		Napoleon invades Russia but is forced to retreat
		The Adamses' daughter Louisa Catherine Adams dies
1814	★	Francis Scott Key writes "The Star-Spangled Banner"
		Napoleon abdicates and goes into exile
		John Quincy Adams leaves St. Petersburg and helps negotiate the Treaty of Ghent that ends the War of 1812
1815	★	Andrew Jackson wins the Battle of New Orleans after the War of 1812 has officially ended

Louisa Adams leaves St. Petersburg and goes to Paris

Napoleon returns to France, rules for 100 days, loses the Battle of Waterloo, and is sent into permanent exile

John Quincy Adams is named U.S. minister to England, and the Adamses move to London

1816 ★ James Monroe is elected president

1817 ★ John Quincy Adams becomes U.S. secretary of state, and the Adamses move to Washington, D.C.

1818 ★ United States and Great Britain agree on a permanent border between the United States and part of Canada at the 49th parallel

1819 ★ United States buys Florida from Spain

1820 ★ James Monroe is reelected president

1823 ★ Monroe Doctrine proclaims the Americas off-limits to European powers

1825 ★ John Quincy Adams becomes president after a disputed election

Erie Canal opens, connecting New York City to cities on the Great Lakes

1826 ★ John Adams and Thomas Jefferson die on July 4

1828 ★ John Adams marries Mary Catherine Hellen in the White House

Andrew Jackson is elected president

Noah Webster's *The American Dictionary of the English Language* is published

1829 ★ *Encyclopedia Americana,* the first U.S. encyclopedia is published

Englishman James Smithson leaves money to found the Smithsonian Institution in Washington, D.C.

George Washington Adams dies

1830 ★ John Quincy Adams is elected to the U.S. House of Representatives from Massachusetts and is reelected every two years until his death

1831 ★ The Adamses move back to Washington, D.C.

1832 ★ Andrew Jackson is reelected president

1833	★	Oberlin College becomes the first to admit women
1834	★	The Adamses' son, John Adams, dies
1836	★	Martin Van Buren is elected president
1837	★	Economic depression spreads throughout the United States
1839	★	Spanish slave ship *Amistad* lands in Connecticut
1840	★	William Henry Harrison is elected president
1841	★	President Harrison dies a month after taking office
		John Tyler becomes president
		John Quincy Adams successfully argues before the Supreme Court the case in favor of freeing the slaves on board the *Amistad*
1844	★	James Polk is elected president
1846	★	United States declares war on Mexico with John Quincy Adams voting against the war
		Oregon Territory is divided between the United States and Great Britain at the 49th parallel
1848	★	Treaty of Guadalupe Hidalgo ends the Mexican War and gives most of the present-day Southwest to the United States
		First U.S. women's rights meeting is held in Seneca Falls, New York
		Gold is discovered in California
		John Quincy Adams dies on February 23 in the Speaker's Room of the U.S. House of Representatives
1849	★	Thousands of people take part in the California gold rush
		Elizabeth Blackwell becomes the first woman in the world to receive a medical degree
1850	★	Zachary Taylor dies and Millard Fillmore becomes president
		National Women's Rights Convention is held in Worchester, Massachusetts
1852	★	Harriet Beecher Stowe's *Uncle Tom's Cabin* is published
		Louisa Catherine Johnson Adams dies on May 15

Fast Facts about
Louisa Catherine Johnson Adams

Born: February 12, 1775, in London, England

Died: May 15, 1852, in Washington, D.C.

Burial Site: Quincy, Massachusetts

Parents: Joshua Johnson and Catherine Nuth Johnson

Education: Catholic convent school in France where she learned to speak fluent French and became interested in Greek and astronomy; boarding school in England; lifelong love of reading and writing

Marriage: To John Quincy Adams on July 26, 1797, until his death on February 23, 1848

Children: George Washington Adams (1801–1829), John Adams (1803–1834), Charles Francis Adams (1807–1886), Louisa Catherine Adams (1811–1812)

Places She Lived: London, England (1775–1778, 1783–1797, 1815–1817); Nantes, France (1778–1783); Berlin (1797–1801); Quincy, Massachusetts (1801–1803, 1829–1831); Washington, D.C. (1803–1808, 1817–1829, 1831–1852); Boston, Massachusetts (1808–1809); St. Petersburg, Russia (1809–1815); Paris, France (1815)

Major Achievements:

⁕ When her husband was secretary of state, acted as his secretary in organizing the State Department and held weekly receptions for government officials.

⁕ Was the most traveled First Lady until 1929, having lived in England, France, Prussia, and Russia.

⁕ Began writing *Record of a Life, or My Story* (1825).

⁕ Arranged the wedding of her son, John Adams, to Mary Catherine Hellen, the only White House wedding of a son of a president, February 25, 1828.

⁕ When her husband was a congressman, helped him organize petitions to Congress to end slavery in the United States.

⁕ Began writing her autobiography, *The Adventures of a Nobody* (1840).

⁕ Helped her cook in Washington, D.C., buy her freedom (1846).

Fast Facts about
John Quincy Adams's Presidency

Terms of Office: Elected in 1825; served as the sixth president of the United States from 1825 to 1829

Vice President: John C. Calhoun (1825–1829)

Major Policy Decisions and Legislation:

* Planned a program of canal and road building that would bind the nation together.
* Accepted an invitation to send delegates to the Pan American Conference in Panama and nominated two delegates to the conference, December 1825.
* Worked for a treaty that determined the U.S. border with Mexico, 1828.
* Signed the Tariff Act of 1828, which was called the "Tariff of Abominations" by Southerners.

Major Events:

* President John Quincy Adams appointed Joel Roberts Poinsett as the first U.S. minister, now called ambassador, to Mexico, March 1825. Poinsett introduced to the United States a Mexican plant that was named poinsettia after him.
* The Erie Canal opened on October 26, 1825.
* The General Conference of South American States opened in Panama on March 24, 1826, but the delegates from the United States did not arrive in time, thus causing the conference to fail and adjourn early.
* President John Quincy Adams appointed Robert Trimble as an associate justice of the U.S. Supreme Court, May 9, 1826.
* President John Quincy Adams broke ground for the Chesapeake and Ohio Canal, July 4, 1828.

Where to Visit

Adams National Historic Site
Adams Street
Quincy, Massachusetts 02269-0531
(617) 773-1177

The Capitol Building
Constitution Avenue
Washington, D.C. 20510
(202) 225-3121

Museum of American History of the Smithsonian Institution
"First Ladies: Political and Public Image"
14th Street and Constitution Avenue, N.W.
Washington, D.C. 20560
(202) 357-2008

National Archives
Constitution Avenue
Washington, D.C. 20408
(202) 501-5000

The White House
1600 Pennsylvania Avenue
Washington, D.C. 20500
Visitors' Office: (202) 456-7041

White House Historical Association (WHHA)
740 Jackson Place NW
Washington, D. C. 20503
(202) 737-8292

Online Sites of Interest

Adams National Historic Site, NPF Guide
http://www.gov./adam/
This site contains a description of the Adams National Historic Site, including the Adamses' birthplace, the Old House and Library, the United First Parish Church, and the visitor center

The Amistad Case, NARA
http://www.nara.gov/education/teaching/amistad/home.html
Includes a detailed background of the Amistad case plus documents and teaching activities from the National Archives and Records Administration

The First Ladies of the United States of America
http://www2.whitehouse.gov/WH/glimpse/firstladies/html/firstladies.html
A portrait and biographical sketch of each First Lady plus links to other White House sites

Internet Public Library, Presidents of the United States (IPL POTUS)
http://www.ipl.org/ref/POTUS
An excellent site with much information on John Quincy Adams, including personal information and facts about his presidency; many links to other sites including biographies, historical documents, other internet resources, and much more

Quincy, Mass.com
http://quincymass.com/
Includes a map of the city, a photo library with pictures of the John Adams home, gardens, and library, a city directory, a calendar of events, and more

The White House
http://www.whitehouse.gov/WH/Welcome.html
Information about the current president and vice president; White House history and tours; biographies of past presidents and their families; a virtual tour of the historic building, current events, and much more

The White House for Kids
http://www.whitehouse.gov/WH/kids/html/kidshome.html
Includes information about White House kids, past and present; famous "First Pets," past and present; historic moments of the presidency; and much more

For Further Reading

Carrion, Esther. *The Empire of the Czars*. Chicago: Childrens Press, 1994.

Clinton, Susan M. *First Ladies*. Cornerstones of Freedom series. Chicago: Childrens Press, 1994.

Fisher, Leonard E. *The White House*. New York: Holiday House, 1989.

Gormley, Beatrice. *First Ladies*. New York: Scholastic, Inc., 1997.

Gould, Lewis L. (ed.). *American First Ladies: Their Lives and Their Legacy*. New York: Garland Publishing, 1996.

Guzzetti, Paula. *The White House*. Parsippany, N. J.: Silver Burdett Press, 1995.

Kent, Deborah. *The White House*. Chicago: Childrens Press, 1994.

Kent, Zachary. *John Quincy Adams: Sixth President of the United States*. Encyclopedia of Presidents. Chicago: Childrens Press, 1987.

Klapthor, Margaret Brown. *The First Ladies*. 8th edition. Washington, D.C.: White House Historical Association, 1995.

Lindsay, Rae. *The Presidents' First Ladies*. New York: Franklin Watts, 1989.

Marrin, Albert. *Napoleon and the Napoleonic Wars*. New York: Viking, 1991.

Mayo, Edith P. (ed.). *The Smithsonian Book of the First Ladies: Their Lives, Times, and Issues*. New York: Henry Holt, 1996.

Sauvain, Philip. *Waterloo*. Great Battles and Sieges series. New York: New Discovery Books, 1993.

Zeinert, Karen. *The Amistad Slave Revolt and American Abolition*. North Haven, Conn.: Linnet Books, 1997.

Index

Page numbers in **boldface type** indicate illustrations

Photo Identifications

Cover: Official White House portrait of Louisa Catherine Johnson Adams
Page 8: Louisa in 1797, the year she married John Quincy Adams
Page 12: A miniature portrait of Louisa as a young woman
Page 28: Louisa as First Lady
Page 40: Czar Alexander I
Page 54: Louisa's mother-in-law, Abigail Adams
Page 66: First Lady Louisa Catherine Johnson Adams and President John Quincy Adams, official White House portraits
Page 78: The Old Home of John and Abigail Adams and their descendants, including Louisa and John Quincy Adams
Page 90: Congressman John Quincy Adams in his later years

Photo Credits©

About the Author

Ann Heinrichs grew up in Arkansas and lives in Chicago. She is the author of more than twenty books for children and young adults on American, Asian, and African history and culture. Her other credits range from classical music critic to advertising copywriter. Ann's books in the Encyclopedia of First Ladies series represent her first foray into biography. Studying the personal diaries, memoirs, and letters of these exceptional women gave her a heartfelt appreciation for their difficult but fascinating lives and times.